Wandering Life's Trails

by
Robert F. Daniels
Poet Laureate

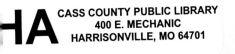

Wandering Life's Trails

Copyright © 2002 by Robert F. Daniels

Library of Congress
Cataloging in Publication Data

ISBN 0-7951-0478-2

Manufactured in The United States of America by
Watermark Press
6 Gwynns Mill Court
Owings Mills, MD 21117
410-654-0400

Dedication

For my wife Suzanne
A gracious lady and a
staunch companion

Success and Happiness

Robert J. Daniels

Us

Loving and caring,
Happy or blue
Together we're sharing
Whatever we do.
Happy together,
Lonesome apart,
I'll love you forever
With all of my heart.
The start of a story
The lives of us two,
A moment of glory
For me and my Sue.

Robert F. Daniels

Beauty

As elusive as a fleeting smile,
As broad as the vagabond sea,
Deep in thought we ponder a while
On beauty and the things that we see.

The paintings and pictures beautific
By masters fulfilling their goal,
The melodious movement of music
Add beauty and depth to the soul.

The wonder and wisdom of nature,
Her scenes majestic to view,
The peace and serenement and pleasure
Of seeing their contrast and hue.

A song of a bird in the Springtime,
The sight of a deer at the brook:
There is beauty for all of us sometime
If we'd only remember to look.

The Mountain Man

When ye think ye of the mountains and the long past days of yore
From Yella stones great fountains out to our western shore,
Don't furget the mountain breed and the shinin' times they'd greet,
Makin' do with what they need and makin' friends
with who they meet.
When ye've trapped those icy rivers and ye've wintered all alone,
When just thinkin' gives ye shivers, then
High Lonesome is ye'r home.

I'll be fetchin' up my plunder when I trade those beaver plews.
There'll be a rowdy time by thunder when
we make the Rendezvous.
There'll be Ol' Mose and Lucian they'll all be rank and wild,
It'll be a grand reunion for my woman and this child.
I'll do some extra talkin' cuz I've panned a little gold,
I'll fetch me up a Hawken, finest gun so I've been told.
Best we gather up our plunder and get ready to head back,
Be times it makes you wonder how ye fit it in the pack.

If ye'd climb the highest peak and drop way down the other side
Ye'd find the valley that ye seek where our cabin does abide.
Ye could do a little fishin' or maybe try your hand at gold,
Or ye might just set there wishin' ye'd been born in days of old.
If ye want to stay awhile ye'd find the peacefulness just fine
And ye'd always have a smile when ye recall those shinin' times.

Mythological

In days of yore a God named Thor
Came down to Earth and fought a war
With thunder bolt and lightning rod;
A vengeful figure was this God.

He struck with a fury compounded by hate
Like the demons from Hell and a wrath that wouldn't wait.
He killed and destroyed with a violent urge
While the wind re-echoed its doleful dirge.
He twisted and turned and relentlessly sought,
Destruction of Earth was his only thought.

Then gentle Venus, God of love,
Sent by Ogden, from above
Came to Earth, with all her grace.
As the mighty warrior saw her face
He put down his thunder and lightning rod
And that was the end of the warring God.

Dreams Of Yesterday

Shattered dreams of yesterday
Will haunt me through the years,
An aching heart and loneliness
Reflect my many tears.

Empty arms and memories
Since you've gone away,
My tangled thoughts are intertwined
With dreams of yesterday.

With gentle face all lined with love
You'd greet me at the door.
Your tender kiss and warm embrace,
I'd love you even more.

Your beauty like the morning dawn,
The happiness we shared,
A lusty love you freely gave
Each knowing how we cared.

Then one day you slipped away
On an angel's wings,
With smiling face you lay at rest
And the torment sorrow brings.

Shattered dreams of yesterday
Will haunt me through the years,
An aching heart and loneliness
Reflect my many tears.

Empty arms and memories
Since you've gone away,
My tangled thoughts are intertwined
With dreams of yesterday.

The Isle Of Erin

Oh, for the twinkle of stars that are shining over Tralee
And the smell of the ocean breeze as it drifts in off the sea,
The joyous people's lives and the brilliant colors I've seen,
The deep, deep blue of the skies and all the shades of the green.
My thoughts are of Ireland's shores, where I am longing to be.

From the banks of the Cliffs of Moher, to Dublin's Irish Sea,
From the giant's wondrous stairs to the beautiful town of Tralee,
The majestic castle ruins and the walls that are made of stone,
The melodious people's songs in all the towns I have known
Leaves a yearning in my heart that keeps calling, calling to me.

The Pioneer

He picked up his musket, his flint, and his knife
And turned his face westward toward hardship and strife,
From out of the wilderness he hewed a new life
And from somewhere beyond, a girl for his wife.

Together they tamed that desolate land,
The hardships they faced they both understand.
The children were born, both rugged and strong,
Many settlers arrived with their families along.

They settled this country, so wild and free,
They built churches and towns and as far as you'd see
There were cornfields and pastures, in town there's a crowd,
"But my freedom's not gone," that pioneer vowed,

So, he picked up his musket, his flint, and his knife
And turned his face westward toward hardship and strife.

Silver Wedding Day

Each year that passes is a precious stone
To be saved and cherished and put away.
Around each gem we've built our home
As we celebrate our wedding day.

Our love grows deeper and more fulfilled
As we gather gems with each passing year.
Our lives grow fuller and happier still
Just knowing the other is always near.

Now our gems are all polished to a silvery hue
And held together in a single mold
To be saved with the others as we start anew;
As the silver begins to turn to gold.

Rock Of Time

Unmoved it stands, this Rock of Time, throughout Eternity,
The seconds pass as grains of sand into infinity.
Ageless ancient Rock of Time, everlasting and sublime,
The years will come, the years go by, and still this Rock of Time.

Eternal Rock unmoved by man, unyielding in his hands
Timeless march engulfs man's life within its flowing sands,
Relentless space evolving down a predetermined line,
The Ages come, the Ages go, and still this Rock of Time.

Vietnam

The rabble, the rubble, destruction of war,
The dirt, the blood, and the fears,
The echo of fighting from Saigon's near shores,
The heartbreak, the sorrow, the tears.

Each knoll that we take and endeavor to keep,
Our friends that lay dead on the way,
The innocent victims and mothers who weep
Are all in the price we must pay.

Desolation of war in a faraway land
From Communist terror release
Is the price we must pay so Vietnam can stand
With freedom, honor, and peace.

Crossroads To Success

The weight of the world as it rests on my shoulders
Is driving me down this endless road,
But knowing one spark within me still smolders
Gives me the strength to carry my load.

I'm going to build me a dream
And make it come true,
And then it will seem
That I've never been blue.

Gonna catch me a cloud
That goes ridin' by
And oh, I'll be proud
Way up there in the sky.

Gonna find me a love
And lead a good life,
The lights shining above,
What a beautiful wife.

But if you float with the tide
You may go drifting by,
We could have been side by side
Way up here in the sky.

You can catch you a dream
And make it come true
And then it will seem
That you've never been blue.

First Love Lost

Like violets blooming in the lane
Washed by softly falling rain,
Forget the sorrow and the pain
And let the sun come out again.

A page in time will dry your tear,
With thoughtfulness your mind will clear.
Your memories are always near,
It's all in growing up, my dear.

Your tender heart will find a way
To find true love another day,
So brush away those tears and pray.
The hurt was not in vain today.

Footsteps Of The Lord

Come walk a little way with me dear Jesus,
Show me which road I need to go.
Help me find the way,
With humble words I pray,
My love for You is all I know.

I'll follow in the footsteps of my Lord,
I'll follow in the footsteps of my Lord.
Let my voice be heard,
I want to spread Your word.
I'll follow in the footsteps of my Lord.

Let me walk a little way with you sweet Jesus,
Down that lonesome road to Calvary
Where You were crucified.
For me You lived and died;
Give me help I pray on bended knee.

I'll follow in the footsteps of my Lord,
I'll follow in the footsteps of my Lord.
Let my voice be heard,
I want to spread Your word.
I'll follow in the footsteps of my Lord.

Please guide me through this life dear Savior
Give me strength to follow where You lead.
Let my heart be true
So I can be with You,
Your help will give me grace and sanctity.

I'll follow in the footsteps of my Lord,
I'll follow in the footsteps of my Lord.
Let my voice be heard,
I want to spread Your word.
I'll follow in the footsteps of my Lord.

Discrimination

Ripped by the roots from his native soil,
Brought to a new and distant land,
Doomed to a desolate life of toil,
He's as important as a grain of sand.

Courts ruled him chattel for a hundred years.
A war was won to free his soul.
His life is still a valley of tears
Just because his face is black as coal.

Ours is Justice and Equality
For every man in the human race,
A land of Opportunity
If yours is not an ebony face.

Now rejected by his native land
A constant hunger where'er he looks,
His living earned by toiling hand,
His hunger for the things in books.

Small are the wants of the Negro folk
To hold up his head as he walks by,
Released for all time of his terrible yoke
To live like a man and not reason why.

The Snowstorm

The night was cold and dreary
And the trees had shed their leaves,
The snowflakes fell with fury
Whipped by a sudden breeze.
The world was dead and empty
As nature spread her shroud of white
And the snowflakes still kept falling
On that cold and savage night.
Driven as by desperation,
Frantic as they knifed the air,
Until they'd reached their destination
Then lay softly everywhere.
The wind grew calm and the snowflakes gleamed
As gently on the ground they lay;
The world awoke all fresh and clean
Ready for another day.

Robert F. Daniels

Eulogy On Sir Winston Churchill

An emblem V – for victory,
A symbol of his name,
He shaped the course of destiny
And humbly bore his fame.

His wisdom lives eternally.
Everlasting was his youth.
His moral fiber – Loyalty
In Country, King, and Truth.

A Nation welded by his faith
In Freedom, Peace, and Love,
A guiding beacon in his wraith
Reflecting from above.

A Last Lament

Singing songs and telling jokes
And drinking their whiskey straight,
When out of the din there came a croak
From a feller' as sudden as fate.

I'm poor and I'm tired of this life I've led,
All this rotgut and hussies in red,
And them that aims in the gambling games
To clean you of all that you've had.

I'm sick of the greed and the whiskery breed
That hangs out in this honky tonk heap,
Of the money I've spent and how it all went
For a life that is bawdy and cheap.

Oh, I've rode with the worst, I've robbed and I've cursed
And I've killed me an Injun or two,
I've held up some trains for material gains
And my virtues, they've been mighty few.

But now I'm all done, gonna hang up my gun
And get out of this honky tonk dive,
Gonna ride a new road and carry my load
And be thankful that I'm still alive.

Then he put down a buck, that he said was for luck,
And turned to go with a lurch,
When a hussy in red stopped him and said
"Bye, Reverend, see you in church!"

Robert F. Daniels

God's Glory

He is the director of our choir,
Hymns of love our voices raise,
His presence sets our souls on fire
With rapturous melodies of praise.

He is the shining light that leads us
Through darkest days of sin and pain.
It was by His own death that He redeemed us
So we could be with Him once again.

What glorious splendor does await us
When we arrive at heaven's door,
With tenderest love He will embrace us
And we'll be with Him forevermore.

Forty And Found

Forty and found said the fellow in town,
Forty a month and grub is free.
I came from nowhere and for nowhere I'm bound,
Just drifting for the sights that I see.

Food and forty a month and found
You can work by the month if you choose,
But you seldom get the chance to get down into town
And look at all the time that you lose.

Forty a month is just cash that you need
For the stake to be on your way,
If you belong to that wanderin' breed
Just driftin' for the joy of each day.

Reflections

Little boy with innocent grace,
Wondering ways and shining face,
Expectant questions why and how,
Wanting facts and answers now,
Eagerly learning all he can,
Impatient to become a man.

Somehow the years have passed him by.
Ambitious man with goal so high,
He sees the irony nature wrought.
Memories are his idle thoughts
Backward where the years have led
From boyhood thoughts of what's ahead.

The Rose

I see within a single rose
A dignity fulfilled
It lifts its head as though it knows
God placed it there — and still

Its fragrant beauty is for man,
His sight and scent and soul,
A blueprint of the Master Plan
For life's Eternal goal.

The Wrath Of God

Repent! Ye Nations torn with strife –
Amend thy unholy path,
Atone thy sins, and honor life,
Or expect to face My Wrath.

Reject thy wealth, oh greedy man,
Admit thy wrongful deeds.
Redeem thy soul while you still can.
Eternal art thou needs.

Forget thy petty spiteful goals;
Project thy heart to me.
Erase the blackness from thy soul;
Reflect on Calvary.

Confront thy foe with open heart,
Expressing brother love.
Accept thy faith and take a part.
I'm judging from above.

Soul Repressed

A man's emotions dark and deep
Locked behind an iron mask,
Relaxing only when asleep —
He won't admit them if you ask,
For men would scoff and call him fool
And say he lives a dreamer's dream.
His soul was wrought to be God's tool.
A man's ambitions are his dreams.
He needs to think and feel and love;
To tell his family of his cares,
To know there is a God above
With whom his dreams are always shared.

The Little Drummer Boy

Divided families joined the fight
For the cause they felt was right.
Despairing wives and mothers pray
They'll all be home again someday,
While far away at dawn's first light

The rolling thunder of the guns
Bespoke a battle just begun.
Advancing lines of Blue and Gray,
A battalion Chaplain knelt to pray
Beneath a pleasant summer sun.

Relentless shriek of shot and shell
Like fury from the mouth of Hell,
The tattered Rebel line withdrew
Before the onslaught of Blue
As the crescendo rose and fell.

The savage slash of naked steel,
The torment that the wounded feel,
The dead and dying all around,
Consecrated hallowed ground,
A bugle charge began to peel.

The Drummer Boy picked up the beat
Amid a thousand marching feet.
REGROUP, REGROUP the drumbeat said;
They followed as the Drummer led
Into the battle's searing heat.

The steady cadence of the drums,
The rolling rumble of the guns,
The air was filled with choking dust
And suddenly a saber thrust.
The Drummer Boy released his drums.

The lad was dealt a mortal blow;
He'd trod the path that heroes know.
He stumbled forward just a pace
As recognition crossed his face,
His gaping wound began to flow.

He fell and coughed, his lips frothed red,
The foe in Blue raised up his head.
My Son, My Son, he clutched him close;
I'm sorry father, for us both,
And then the Drummer Boy was dead.

Cowboys That Lived Yesterday

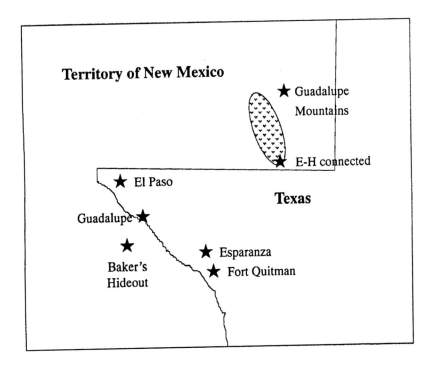

Cowboys That Lived Yesterday

When out of the west I saw him,
On a stallion as red as the sun,
The set of his face looked grim,
As he rode that hoss on the run.

He rode in and asked for water;
I said he might sit a spell.
Said he didn't think he oughta,
But he had a story to tell.

The stranger rode in and asked for water. I pointed out the pump and watering trough. He slid from his saddle and watered his horse. His movements were like a shifting shadow.

He was a well-put-together man. He stood over six foot tall and, at a hundred and seventy pounds, had the look about him like a coiled rattlesnake.

I asked if he might sit a spell and he replied he'd spare a few minutes to give his horse a chance to blow. Mentioned he had a story to tell about a ruckus down across the border in Old Mexico.

John Horton was his name but he'd picked up the handle of Johnny Danger during the war. He'd earned that moniker by breaking through the Blue Belly picket lines and raising all kinds of hell. After the hostilities were over, Johnny drifted back home to the hard times Texas was going through at Waco.

When the scalawags and carpetbaggers got too thick, Johnny and his sidekick Ward Enroe drifted on west to the foothills of the Guadalupe Mountains north of El Paso.

The boys worked hard gathering and branding wild longhorns. Every chance they could they would run wild mustangs for saddle stock and for sale to the Army for cavalry remounts.

Now, six years later, John and Ward were getting fairly well - established with a herd of about thirty-five hundred longhorns and over three hundred head of brood mares and saddle stock. The ranch encompassed twenty-six sections of high mountain summer pasture with winter graze in the foothills.

The E-H Connected always kept about four or five riders, as well as Slats McKee who was the chief camp cook and biscuit roller.

Times generally stayed fairly quiet except for the Indians raising hell now and then. The biggest problem in the country came from Shaker Jake Baker. He claimed he was a preacher, however he spent most of his time raiding wagon trains on the Santa Fe Trail with his band of outlaws.

The Army tried to protect the trail travelers but just couldn't seem to catch up with Shaker Jake's outlaws.

Jake always took his family with him on his forays. His beautiful Mexican wife, Rosa, grew old and worn out with the wild life and constant traveling of those hellions. Late last spring she just gave out and gave up. They found her dead one morning. Their daughter, an only child, was old Jake's pride and joy. Vanessa was nineteen now and more breathtakingly beautiful than her mother had been.

Shaker Jake's band of cutthroats crossed trails with the riders from E-H Connected several times over the years. This came about as they were making their way from raiding the trail to trading with Comancheros. They traded stolen goods and rotgut whiskey for rustled livestock that the Comancheros had collected.

Then, in turn, the Comancheros peddled the rotgut to the Indians for furs and that would get them stirred up.

Johnny mentioned after visiting with Vanessa over the past four or five years, while she was growing up, he'd gotten to know her fairly well. He said he was just beginning to think an awful lot of her.

Last month Johnny and four of the boys were up in the mountains building a trap that they hoped to haze a bunch of promising - looking mustangs that they had spotted.

Ward stayed back at the ranch along with a new rider called Slade Gosner. Latigo West was still hobbling around after a bronco threw him. But he was still able to repair whatever tack needed it, to fill his days.

Well, one morning Ward and Slade were rebuilding the corral fence after the last bunch of wild ones had the rough taken out of them. The sun was about straight up when an Indian family came drifting in on three ponies and an old black mule toting their possibles. They had a pair of boys about six or eight years old.

Ward told Slade to take them on down to the cook shack and see if old Slats could rustle up some grub for them.

While the family followed, Slade went stomping away like he had a poker in his back. Ward recollected that the Indian was a Yaqui Apache cross called Juan Vesquez. Vesquez was might near famous as a tracker. Several times Juan had done jobs for the E-H Connected. As a result, the family was well-known and always welcome. His woman and the boys always traveled wherever they went.

Shortly, Enroe heard a ruckus down by the cook shack and went drifting that way to see what was up.

It seems that Gosner brought the grub he'd gotten from McKee and dumped it in a pile on a table out front. Gosner then said, "There, you damn redskins are lower than a pack of dogs. So you can just root right in like a bunch of dogs."

As Ward approached, he said, "That's no way to treat a man. Put a hobble on your tongue."

Gosner than replied, "I'm not cozying up to a bunch of gut-eaters to satisfy you or any man. If you think I am, just to kiss your hind end, you better get yourself another think."

Enroe replied, "I'll have no small-minded nasty-tempered riders on my crew." With that Ward threw him a few dollar bills and told him to go fetch his bedroll, saddle, bronco, and be off the ranch in ten minutes.

As Slade left, Ward got a bucket of water from the pump so the family could wash off the trail dust. He then had Slats set out a decent meal for the family.

Johnny and the boys rode in three days later with fifteen fine-looking mares for the breeding herd, once they had been gentled.

By then Latigo was back riding again. That evening when he rode in he said that he had been checking the stock. He said that he had ridden down by the lower gap and it appears a bunch of saddle stock had been driven through it. After working the breaks and arroyos Latigo reckoned they were missing nigh onto forty head.

Enroe said, "and I can about tell you where they are. A buck to a broken cinch strap, I'll bet Gosner drove them away after I drove him off. If the Comancheros don't have them now, then Shaker Jake Baker does."

Come first light the following morning Johnny was in the saddle riding for the lower gap to pick up the trail of the rustled stock. By late afternoon he had ridden across the border into Texas and from there the trail curved westerly. By mid-morning the following day, the strong winds had blown enough sand and dust to obliterate the tracks.

Johnny found an arroyo out of the wind and built a small fire. While the coffee was on, he did some tall thinking. He figured eventually old Shaker Baker would end up with the horses regardless of whatever had happened. He knew the general locality of Baker's headquarters, a day or two ride down to Old Mexico, across the Rio Grande. Without knowing anything else he turned his horse south towards Esperanza. Horton knew of a pretty good trail going that way. A couple years earlier he had trailed some saddle stock down that way to Fort Quitman as cavalry remounts. Johnny was hoping to learn something of Shaker Baker's movements when he reached the fort. With any luck in recovering the horses, he hoped to be back to the E-H Connected in a week or ten days.

Late afternoon on the third day, John rode into Fort Quitman. At the command headquarters, Major Lefke told John that one of the patrols had discovered a heavy stock track crossing the Rio Grande about ten miles to the west. Both horse and cattle tracks were evident. The Major had assumed that the tracks had been made by Jake Baker's outfit, but as yet, the patrols hadn't seen anything of the outlaws.

"By the way," Major Lefke said, "that Yaqui tracker Vesquez came drifting in this morning. Maybe he can help you."

Johnny left headquarters to have a look around for Juan and his outfit. They finally got together just as Vesquez was coming out of the Sutler's with an armload of supplies.

It was near sundown so Johnny Danger camped with the Vesquez family just outside the fort. Juan's wife fixed supper while the men hobbled the horses and mule on good graze next to a tiny brook.

By the time they got down to coffee and smokes, Johnny was explaining to Juan about the E-H Connected's horses being run off, and his mission to try to recover them.

After parlaying for awhile, Juan mentioned that he had a pretty fair idea about where Shaker Jake Baker's headquarters were. He felt that with the fresh tracks the Cavalry Patrol had spotted, he could probably find it. He thought it was only about a day or two ride from where they were. Finally, it was agreed that the Vesquez family would stay camped right there while the two men tried to unravel the trail. Without the family along, they would have more freedom of movement and could travel faster.

At first light the following morning, they crossed the river and turned northwesterly. Vesquez's intention was to intercept the trace, if the wind and sand hadn't obliterated it.

After riding most of the day, they came upon a sign in the late afternoon. The sign was spotty, almost wiped out in places and quite plain in others. The trail angled off to the southwest.

At sundown they made camp and Juan felt that sometime tomorrow they would find the Baker place.

Early the next afternoon they came upon a small knoll that overlooked a tiny valley. It was an emerald green oasis of beauty amid the arid backdrop of the surrounding territory. They knew at once they had found Jake Baker's hideout.

As they descended into the valley, they became aware of the stillness surrounding the ranch buildings. They realized as they approached that it must be right at siesta time.

On hearing a screen door shut they saw the girl, Vanessa, walking toward an artesian well with a water bucket. Johnny told Vesquez, "If we ease on over to the corner of the blacksmith shop we should be able to attract her attention without making much noise." Just as they got in position, the girl was walking past at only about forty feet away.

Johnny called softly, "Vanessa." Startled, she looked up, then recognized him and came over to where the men were standing.

As she approached, Johnny noticed that her face was swollen and one eye blackened. As they stepped back out of sight, Johnny asked her what had happened.

Vanessa then told a horror story of abuse by several of the hoodlums. After several years of lewd remarks and sly looks, just lately things started getting more personal. When she resisted the advances of the latest would-be Romeo, he began to slap her around. Her father, Jake, was no help she said. He claimed she was swishing her skirts and teasing the men deliberately and whatever she got she had coming to her. She was completely terrorized and had nowhere to turn for help. Vanessa then told the men that this was the sort of life her mother had to live before it killed her. She was determined to escape any way she could and begged Johnny to help her.

Just about then Johnny gave up all thoughts of recovering those forty head of horses he'd been trailing. He was determined to help her if he could.

After thinking a minute, Johnny said, "Our horses are worn down pretty fine as we've come a long way. I don't think we would stand much of a chance to get away if your dad's bunch grabbed fresh horses."

Vanessa said, "We could take Dad's Red Racer. There isn't a horse alive that could catch him." She said he was a hot-blooded stallion that old Shaker Jake had brought up from Mexico City. "He's in a stall in the barn right now," she mentioned.

"Juan, will you keep our backs covered until we make it to the barn and grab the horse and get away?"

Juan agreed and then said that as long as it was still siesta time he could cover the yard with his blow gun. We may get lucky and pull it off with nobody stirring.

Juan's blow gun shot darts that he had poisoned with his own concoction. The darts would paralyze in just a few seconds and kill within a couple of minutes. With their plans made, they didn't wait any longer. Vesquez was in a good position right where he was. By going along the back side of the blacksmith shop, Vanessa and Johnny had about one hundred and fifty feet in the open to get to the barn. Johnny Danger took her hand and they traveled fast across the open gap and were at the barn door within seconds. Danger grabbed the door and slid through it like a shadow with the girl following him.

As he came through the door, Johnny Danger saw a Vanquero leaning against the wall of a stall just inside. The rider had a smoke in his mouth and was handling a bridle. In that instant the outlaw dropped the bridle and went for his gun. Desperate to avoid any noise, Johnny Danger's knife was in his hand by the time he'd traveled the ten feet to where the gunslinger stood. Johnny hit him hard and fast. He opened up the outlaw like a butchered beef. The man was dead before he hit the ground.

At the same time he saw a movement in the corner of his eye. Johnny Danger whirled down and away and the thrown knife missed him. As he threw his own knife, Johnny heard a small cry behind him. His knife caught the outlaw in the throat and he went down.

When he glanced at Vanessa he saw that she had caught the blade in the lower ribs on her right side. Johnny ran to the tack room where the second man lay dead. After recovering his knife he grabbed an old shirt thrown across a saddle.

He was back with Vanessa within seconds. After removing the knife he made a pad of his bandanna and swiftly placed it over the wound and tied it in place with strips torn from the old shirt. That was about all he could do for her. Although it looked bad, he knew that they wouldn't be able to find a Saw Bones until they got back across the border.

Johnny Danger spotted the red stud a couple stalls down and that animal was something to see. He weighed better than thirteen hundred pounds and stood at least seventeen hands high. The stallion looked like he was really built for speed and distance.

After bridling the stud, Johnny slapped on a saddle that hung on a nearby peg. He then grabbed an extra saddle blanket to wrap up the girl and got her into the saddle. He led the stud over to the door, kicked it open and vaulted up behind Vanessa all in one sudden move.

As they came through the door his heels came down hard and in three jumps that Red Racer was going flat out.

His gun came out and he fired several shots at the outlaws pouring out of the bunkhouse. Johnny noticed that Vesquez had been busy also, as he could see three men down in the yard already.

Johnny Danger never knew it, but between him and Vesquez they downed seven of the wild bunch that day, including the ramrod.

Knowing Juan as well as he did, Johnny knew that he'd drift back into the wilderness and then nobody could catch him. John figured that, in a couple days, Vesquez would rendezvous back at Fort Quitman with his family.

As they rode out of that pretty little valley they held their pace for half an hour or more. By then he realized what a hell of a horse he was straddling. He pulled the stud back into a lope, a gait he could hold all day, and the animal was still traveling faster than many horses do at a gallop.

> They finally got to the horses
> And headed north on the run
> Just ahead of the outlaw forces
> On a stallion as red as the sun.

The jolting ride was especially hard on Vanessa but it couldn't be helped. Right after leaving the valley she lost consciousness.

By heading north for the Guadalupe Crossing of the Rio Grande, Johnny figured it would be the shortest distance and they could make it in about three more hours. All he could do was hang on and hope.

About dusk they ran into a small stream, so Johnny stopped a few minutes to water the Red Racer and give him a chance to blow.

He got Vanessa laid down on the ground and fetched some water in his hat. After he wet her lips and bathed her face she showed signs of recovering consciousness. Johnny worked with her and finally got her to swallow a little water. By now she was running a fever and her color didn't look good. After getting a little more water into her, Johnny decided that the best thing they could do was to get across the river and find a pill roller. Once again they got settled back on the stud and pushed north. A little while later, just as Johnny could see the lights of Guadelupe off to the right, Vanessa gave a little gasp, trembled and then went limp. Johnny stopped the horse and checked her. Nothing more could be done: she was dead.

With a hard knot in his belly, Johnny kept the Red Racer headed for the Rio Grande.

They hit the river just before midnight. After crossing, John rode on for a couple more miles. Off to the side he noticed a knoll that rose up about twenty or thirty feet. After riding to the top, he found some mesquite trees and there he picketed the stallion. There at the very top of the knoll, using one of his boots as a shovel he dug out enough sand to make a decent grave for the girl he had learned to love. He wrapped her in the saddle blanket and laid her gently in the sandy grave. After saying a few words about the hard struggle on earth and the peaceful happiness of heaven, he closed the grave.

In exhaustion he then fell asleep by the grave.

At dawn the next morning Johnny looked around and found several rocks which he placed over the grave to discourage the varmints.

Nothing more could be done so he saddled the stud and headed off northeasterly toward home. Johnny figured he had about a three day ride ahead of him to get home. After traveling some especially arid country, he finally spotted a cabin about midafternoon.

As he rode in he saw an old codger sitting on the front porch. Johnny asked if he might have some water. The old man invited him to sit a spell.

> As he finished his story he mounted,
> The stallion as red as the sun,
> A soft ADIOS resounded,
> And then he left on the run.

The End

Cowboys That Lived Yesterday

The evenin' sun was just sinkin',
At the end of a hot Texas day,
And I was just sittin' there thinkin'
Of the cowboys that lived yesterday.

When out of the west I saw him,
On a stallion, red as the sun.
The set of his face looked grim,
As he rode that hoss on the run.

He rode in and asked for water,
I said that he might sit a spell,
Said that he didn't think he oughtta,
But he had a story to tell.

He'd just come north from the border,
And only escaped with his life.
He kidnapped an outlaw's daughter,
And fought his way clear with his knife.

He loved that Mexican lady,
Her beauty could drive a man mad,
But they got caught by her daddy,
And the outlaw band that he had.

They finally got to the horses,
And headed up north on the run,
Just ahead of the outlaw forces,
On a stallion red as the sun.

Robert F. Daniels

As they rode north for the river,
They escaped from the violent fray.
With a knife wound someone gave her,
In his arms she died late that day.

He brought her with him to the border,
And there in the soft Texas sand,
He buried his Mexican lover,
On a knoll by the Rio Grande.

As he finished his story he mounted
The stallion red as the sun;
A soft "ADIOS" resounded,
And then he left on the run.

As I sit there and still remember
The one that just rode away,
In front of the campfire's embers,
And the cowboys that lived yesterday.

Our Redeemer

I walked the path to Calvary, that Jesus
walked that day,
I saw His tomb, the sepulchre and the
stone He rolled away.
when He was risen from the dead, after
being crucified,
His suffering redeemed our sins, our
souls are sanctified.
His mother's heart was torn in two on
that dreadful day.
I walked the path to Calvary. He guided
me the way.

The Wrong To Be Right

Resentment of Darkness rejecting the light.
The face of a crowd avoiding a fight,
The pathos of blindness refusing to sight
Is human advancement the wrong to be right.

Confusing with chaos to magnify fright,
To reign by destruction and rule by your might,
Corrupting the concepts that wisdom excite
Is human advancement the wrong to be right.

Compare your ambitions with Tom Edison's light,
How Benjamin Franklin once flew a kite,
And Perpetual freedom for which we will fight
Is human advancement the wrong to be right.

Missouri's Seasons

The dogwood that's blooming on top of the hill, .
The meadow larks soft melodious trill,
The daffodils brightness by my window sill,
The fragrance of springtime is always a thrill.

The whip-poor-will calling a song to his mate,
The fireflies flicker when evening is late,
The roses are climbing by my garden gate,
The hot hazy days of summer are great.

The bursting of color, leaves magically fall,
The high flying geese and their echoing call,
The quail that are sunning themselves by the wall,
The brisk autumn breezes as temperatures fall.

The snowflakes that fall with astonishing grace,
The whiteness that changes the Earth's haggard face,
The window is painted all frosty with lace,
The contrast makes this a most wonderful place.

Aftermath

One day in May the sun didn't shine,
An enveloping void of timelessness.
The fresh clean air like a fine old wine
Corrupted into uselessness.

The bustling sounds of a busy earth
As it grasped each day as a tool of time,
Aggressive lands end their natural worth,
Ascended the path that all leaders climb.

Then, the clashing wills of the dominant few
And the horror that spread in the following days,
The bombs that fell and their residue
Darkened the sun and her brilliant rays.

Blackness and death and horror and hate;
The quiet that followed was thunderously still.
Destroyed were the wonders we strove to create,
Forgotten the goals we tried to fulfill.

Fulfillment

The love of a woman in the heart of a man
Are two things on earth that go hand in hand;
The thoughtful conviction of life's future plan
And the love of a woman in the heart of a man.

The love of a woman in the heart of a man,
Expanding in stature from the time it began,
Gaining fulfillment throughout their life's span;
The love of a woman in the heart of a man.

The love of a woman in the heart of a man,
The tender compassion, the fire unfanned,
The peace and contentment they both understand:
The love of a woman in the heart of a man.

Robert F. Daniels

Even-tide

With the haze upon the meadows
And the shadows in the Glen
The peaceful hush of evening
Is with us once again.

The solitude of stillness
And the quiet summer night,
A muted cry of mourning
By a winging dove in flight.

The humble call of crickets
As the stars peep out one by one,
And the thoughtful contemplation
When our daily toil is done.

Forgive Me

Forgive me for the dreams we made together
Which will never be, but only dreams grown cold.
Forgive me for the love I said would last forever
That dimmed with time and gradually grew cold.

Forgive me for the lies which I have spoken
And for pretending that we would always be the same,
Forgive me for vows that I have broken,
And for all the tomorrows that never came.

Memories will haunt me now forever
Of all the joy and happiness you gave.
Those empty words which I can tell you never
As with tear-dimmed eyes I walk now from your grave.

Robert F. Daniels

The Wandering Traveler

Listen, you can hear him!
He's on the move again.
I always wait his coming
Since I can't remember when.
He sweeps around the corner
And out across the plain,
You can see the way he's going
By the ripple of the grain.
He's the wandering traveler,
My private name for him,
You can never see him coming
But only where he's been.
Sometimes he hurries swiftly
Like a charging steed on high
Rushing onward quickly
As he breathes across the sky.
At times he moves so quietly
You can hardly tell he's come,
Other times he's sprightly
Like a deer upon the run.
I wonder where he came from
And what sights he's taken in.
I wonder where it all will end,
This journey of the wind.

The Blessed Trinity

Glorification of the Trinity
Hallelujah, Songs of Praise,
The Grandeur of their Divinity,
Their abiding Love throughout our days,
The precious Grace and Unity
And Blessed forgiveness of our sinful ways.

The Father's power and majestic grandeur
As the Creator of the Universe,
The wonderous beauty and mighty splendor
Of the beauty He created here on Earth,
The harmony and awesome wonder
And the reassurance of our worth.

Our Savior came to walk among us
The Redeemer preaching Love and Peace,
Then came His death by crucifixion
As He gave us the Eucharistic feast.
He defeated death by resurrection
As we sing His praises on bended knees.

The Blessed Spirit gives us protection
From Satan's snares by redeeming grace,
He points our lives in a new direction
With Peace and Hope of Eternal Grace.
Our hearts are filled with expectation
Until we meet Him face to face.

The Sanctification of the Trinity,
The Blessed Assurance of their Love,
The Exaltation of the Divinity
With Blessings showered from above,
The abiding graciousness and Unity
From our God; who is pure Love.

Contemplation

Inviting is the shady nook
By a small meandering brook.
Insignificant they say,
But what I dwell upon today.

Where it came from, where it goes,
Why it wanders, no one knows.
Will the bed so soft with sand
Lead it to a promised land?
Do the stones within its path
Cause ripples of indignant wrath?

This brook is like the life of man;
Its length, the years which he has spanned.
The sandy bottom is the force
Projecting Man upon his course,
The stones are troubles in his life,
The ripples represent his strife,
The brook of life keeps flowing on;
The years of Man will soon be gone.

Dawn Greets The Morning

The glimmer of the dawning
As the sun peeps o'er the hill,
The first faint light of morning
Greets the world with all its glory
As each day begins its story
Always different and enchanting,
Master painter and his painting
Splashing color ever skyward
Always radiating outward
From the brilliant shining star
And the clouds that catch the brightness
From the dawn's reflecting lightness
Change their color from their whiteness
To a bright and splendored hue.
As the morning sun grows lighter
The early dawning painter
Puts away his paints and painting
For his daily work is through.

Alone

The eye grows dim, the years are long
The feeble step that once was strong
And knowing that death's door is near
A younger heart, the mind is clear
With remembrance of you.

The hopes and dreams we both have shared
Each knowing how the other cared,
A lasting love keeps living on
Consoling sorrow since you've gone,
And remembrance of you.

The solitude of circumstance that fills
this lonely life,
The passing years and emptiness with which
my mind is rife,
The end is near, be not afraid, I greet it
as a friend,
The strength to cross Eternity when I come
to this road's end
Is in remembrance of you.

Remember How We Used To Be

You smile through the tears while I'm leaving, dear,
While I remember your love through the years.
Your eyes seem to say in their special way,
We'll be together in heaven some day.

All the stars in the skies reflect from your eyes
And the light from above seems to echo our love.
When you whispered, dear, I'd be holding you near;
Just remember how we used to be.

Your heart understands as you take my hand
My love will always be yours to command,
I'll watch over you whenever you're blue,
I'll be by your side 'til your life is through.

All the stars in the skies reflect from your eyes
And the light from above seems to echo our love.
When you whispered, dear, I'd be holding you near;
Just remember how we used to be.

As you knelt to pray I'm slipping away,
If you realize what more can I say?
Love lasts forever if you remember
All the happiness we've had together.

All the stars in the skies reflect from your eyes
And the light from above seems to echo our love.
When you whispered, dear, I'd be holding you near;
Just remember how we used to be.

Christmas Time

Sleigh bells jingle in the night,
Joyous laughter, child's delight,
Church bells calling
Snowflakes falling
Add beauty to the Christmas lights.

Expectations
Celebrations
Whispered secrets
Christmas joy,
Finding gifts for a special someone,
Happiness for each girl and boy.

Wrapping presents,
Burning incense,
Shopping, cooking,
Christmas love.
Blessed Savior brought forgiveness
And redemption from above.

Memoriam

The dark and dismal doom of death,
The tolling of the Chapel bell,
The service told for one who's left
Whom we loved and knew so well.
He was gone in a passing breath;
The only sound is the tolling knell.

The bleak remorseful dress of black
That signified the crowds' respect,
The memories that come pouring back,
A friendship that we can't reject.
Our shattered lives were once intact
And then a death we didn't expect.

We'll miss the friendship of his face
The thoughtless things that he'd condone,
The way he talked with a quiet grace,
His helping hand to all he'd known.
Now he's found his final resting place,
The longest walk he took alone.

Retribution

A life for a life and an eye for an eye,
A lifetime of strife in living a lie,
Redeeming a wrong in condemning a man,
Justice is gone and honor is ban.

Vengeance and hate and obsessions of wrong,
Reason irate and vindication prolonged,
Retribution belongs to a just judge of man
Protecting a strong and honorable land.

The Wind In The Willow

The sparkle of gold that's washed from the sand,
The glitter of diamonds you wear with such grace
Are nothing compared to what love understands
And the beauty of heaven that shines on your face.

The wind in the willow whispers I love you,
Your head on my pillow, I'm holding you near
With moonlight so bright shining upon you
And I realize that you are so dear.

The rumble of thunder, my heart's beating faster
While I lie here and wonder if you understand
That only the lonely know what they're after
And how they are missing the life that we planned.

The wind in the willow whispers I love you,
Your head on my pillow, I'm holding you near
With moonlight so bright shining upon you
And I realize that you are so dear.

As I kiss you softly and then with desire
Your breathing is faster as you cling to me.
As we come together our love is on fire
As we are fulfilling the voice of the tree.

The wind in the willow whispers I love you,
Your head on my pillow, I'm holding you near
With moonlight so bright shining upon you
And I realize that you are so dear.

The wind in the willow whispers I love you
Your head on my pillow, I'm holding you near
With moonlight so bright shining upon you
And I realize that you are so dear.

Trail Town

Late one night in a trail town bar
Two cowpokes, who had traveled far,
Were drinkin' them straight and eyein' the crowd.
It's a lowdown dive, they both avowed,
While an old piano beat out a tune
Of better days in that old saloon.

A big blond floozy with a painted face
Came lumbering up with a buffalo's grace,
She asked, "Would you boys like a song?"
They said, "If it's free we can't go wrong."
Then she huffed away to hustle her trade
And find a mark, so she'd be paid.

The barkeep just kept wiping the bar
And he asked, "Have you boys traveled far?"
"Three months on the trail a-swallowing dust,
Gonna push that herd to market or bust,
River crossings and drizzling rain
And the painted desert where my horse went lame.

Up the mountains and across the Divide
And we find 'this town' on the other side.
It's a terrible jolt to a buckaroo
And I'm happy to say we're just passing through."
Then they downed their drinks and said it's like jail
And headed on out for the lonesome trail.

The Bible

A book of black all worn and aged,
Enduring strength on written page,
A symbolic guide of a future goal
For salvation of the immortal soul.

A cloak of fortitude it wears;
All in need will find it there
Inspiring man throughout his years,
Disparaging solitude and fears.

A valued treasure in my home,
The most important thing I own,
Renewing faith when e'er I look;
It's always there in that old black book.

On Growing Up

My son
Growing up is many things,
A winding route for untried wings;
The path in years is one straight line
Unfolding in the course of time.

Respect the magic of your mind
Devour all knowledge you can find,
Adventure to the land of books.
Enjoy the peace of quiet nooks.

Just place your human values high
And watch life's riches multiply,
Compassion for your fellow man,
Be generous with a helping hand.

It's all in growing up, my son,
You'll find that life has just begun,
Your character will grow sublime
Tempered by the touch of time.

Our World

The sun, the moon, and the stars in the sky
Shine down on earth for both you and I
The wind and the rain and the grass in the dell
The rivers and mountains and all I can tell

Are things that we own awake and asleep
Things that we share — but we never can keep
The sun and the moon and the stars up above
All shine on me and the one that I love

Robert F. Daniels

Heaven's Gift

I'm floating high in the air;
Have you heard the news?
She's got dark curly hair,
When you hold her she coos.
With her perfect form
She's the tiniest Angel,
From the day she was born
Our love for her kindled.
It's like owning a dream
Being blessed from above;
She is our tiny Queen,
We are bursting with love.

Nostalgia

The skies are bluer,
Bluer water
For every native son and daughter.
The fishing's greater,
The highway's straighter
Comin' back to Minnesota
When you're comin' home.

The cooks are greatest,
Little lunches
For all the friends that come in bunches.

The air is cleaner,
The grass is greener
Comin' back to Minnesota
When you're comin' home,
YOU BETCHA'!

Robert F. Daniels

The Berlin Wall

A monument of mute disgrace,
A wall of steel stood in the place
Where East and West were torn apart,
Broken land and bleeding heart;
A crime that history can't erase.

Day by day against the light
Stone by stone it grew in height,
Hate and fear were those first stones,
Year by year the list has grown
Desecrating all that's right.

The protruding pendulum of hate,
The crushing burden of its weight,
Its ponderous swing embrace all
Whose lives are ruled by that bleak wall;
A divided nation's tragic fate.

Mother Teresa's Missionaries Of Charity

Who are these sisters that venture the streets
Bringing God's love to whomever they meet?
They bring help for the homeless and food for the poor
While walking among us and they do so much more,

Provide care for the innocents born with such grace
With tender endearment on each smiling face,
They bring compassion and joy as they venture through life
And offer generosity and love to hardship and strife.

Tenderness and sacrifice they wear with such grace
With the touch of our savior on each smiling face,
Peace blessings and God's love.

Robert F. Daniels

Broken Hearts, Lonesome Nights, And Empty Arms

Broken hearts, lonesome nights, and empty arms.
I was just another victim of your charms.
You left me all alone, with no one to call my own;
You didn't even ask me, you just began to roam.

Broken hearts, lonesome nights, and empty arms.
You make the rules for breaking hearts, then do your harm.
All my kisses leave you cold and you're done with me I'm told
But you'll never find another half as faithful when you're old.

Broken hearts, lonesome nights, and empty arms.
If you get hurt by the fate of someone's charms
You'd see that I was right and you were wrong;
Come back to me where you belong.

And there'll be no more
Broken hearts, lonesome nights, and empty arms.

I Wish "Your Love"

You're always witty, happy, and gay
and especially prim.
How you plan your approach for each day
makes life impossibly grim.

I wish you were wild and wanton and free,
impulsive and eager for love;
Total abandon when you're with me
is the thought that I'm dreamin' of.

The tender sweetness of your love
is beautiful to see,
You surround me whenever I move;
I wish you'd set me free.

I wish you were wild and wanton and free,
impulsive and eager for love;
Total abandon when you're with me
is the thought that I'm dreamin' of.

Never the time or never the way,
even when lights are dim.
I wish somehow you'd learn to play
it's important to him.

I wish you were wild and wanton and free,
impulsive and eager to love;
Total abandon when you're with me
is the thought that I'm dreamin' of.

Robert F. Daniels

You're the perfect woman for my wife
and I guess you'll always be.
I know I'll love you for all my life
if only you'll let me.

I wish you were wild and wanton and free,
impulsive and eager for love;
Total abandon when you're with me
is the thought that I'm dreamin' of.

I wish you were wild and wanton and free,
impulsive and eager for love;
Total abandon when you're with me
is the thought that I'm dreamin' of.

Christmas

Away in a manger
No room for a stranger,
The town was so crowded,
A stable His bed.

The babe lay there sleeping,
The Shepherds were keeping
Watch on our Savior
And the star overhead.

The Angels were singing,
From the East Wise Men bringing
Treasures to honor
Our Redeemer, just born.

Peace reigned the World
O'er that tiny babe curled
Away in a manger –
Our first Christmas Morn.

Robert F. Daniels

Gas Power

The truck got stranded on the road,
Here I'm stuck with a heavy load;
It must be the gas.

The beans were cooking on the stove,
While I'm watching they explode;
It must be the gas.

The furnace shook and then expanded
Four miles away before it landed;
It must be the gas.

The old outhouse way out yonder
Suddenly was blown asunder;
It must be the gas.

Politicians twit and fiddle,
They ride the fence or ride the middle;
It must be the gas.

Blow them up or blow them down,
The power of gas is world renown;
IT IS THE GAS.

God's Gifts

The shifting of the sands of time
That eddy like a dying wind,
The eternal motion of the sea,
The tides that voice their song to me.
Changing shadows, once again
Bring grandeur to a life sublime,
The greatness of our God above
That brings us happiness and love.

The Pharaoh's Bride

The aged Egyptian pharaoh frowned;
Her face in innocence remained benign.
Her wondrous beauty was renowned,
   · In shackles she remained confined
Though proud and tall her eyes looked down.

The pharaoh scowled and then in rage
With wrath he cursed the innocent maid.
From time-worn history came this page
   As the maiden faced him unafraid.
Can a marriage survive 'tween youth and age?

Does a father who gives up his daughter regret
The powers he's gained and favors he knew?
Can a daughter rebel and make them forget
Traditional customs? Her chances are few.
Her sacrificed life is just payment of debt.

Seconds Of Love

There are 60 seconds in every minute.
When you're in love, time's a treasure;
Every second has happiness in it,
Just being with you is a pleasure.

When we're together, time passes so swiftly
But lingers so long when we're parted.
It seems just a second that you've been with me,
When the evening is through, we've just started.

The seconds are passing and changing to minutes,
These hours have gone forever.
Let's break all the clocks, so the seconds will stop
And we'll be always together.

Dreaming

Everyone knew I was dreaming
When I thought that your love could be true,
You lied and I kept on believing
That life could be heaven with you,

Your two-timing me is the end, can't you see?
You'd never be happy I know.
You needn't pretend it won't happen again,
I love you but must let you go.

It's better to leave you forever
Than let you keep making me blue.
Yes, everyone knew I was dreaming
But now I'm not dreaming of you.

Dog Gone

I had a dog that climbed a tree and whistled like a bird.
He couldn't talk and couldn't see and couldn't hear a word.
He'd sit all day and whistle so merrily and gay,
Then one day he disappeared ———— I guess he flew away.

Hands

The love of a mother and soft tender smile
And her gentle hands while holding a child,
The nurse and her patients, their lives in her hands,
The living and dying she both understands,
The hands of our Pastor and Novena's Ovation
Blessing our lives and all of Creation,
The hands of a lover as she touches your face
While holding you close in Love's sweet embrace,
The love of a father and strength of his hands
Protecting and guiding throughout his life's span,
The love of our Savior and touch of His hands
Our existence in Heaven is His to command.
The use of our hands is a gift from above
While the good that they do is a labor of love.

Redeemed

Beat plowshares from your swords,
Fight your battles then with words
Knowing God is always at your side.
End the life of hate and death
And with each avenging breath
Rejecting Hell and Satan as your guide.

Remember how He died
And that our lives are sanctified
With His coming and forgiveness of our sins.
Just glorify the Lord
While remembering His word
As we await His coming once again.

Robert F. Daniels

For Mary Dempsey of Clonmel County Tipperary Ireland

There in the County Tipperary
In the land of the wee folk and fairy
Lived many a Miss
With the touch of God's kiss,
But the fairest of all was sweet Mary.

Old Age Or Else

When you get old and your hair turns grey
Most falls out, but some will stay,
You're getting creaky in the joints
And that is one of the important points.

Remember how it used to be
When you were young and you could see?
You could laugh and jump and run all night
Then the years slipped by and your hair turned white.

Time went by, and you've got the gout,
You're drinking soup cuz you're teeth fell out,
Old age has come and you've lost your voice
But — Just think of the other choice!

Robert F. Daniels

Mother's Day

Who wiped our tears and calmed our fears,
Who nurtured us throughout the years,
Who lights the lamp of love she'd share,
Whose hand to give us guiding care?
Of course — It was our Mother.

Day of days
For songs of praise
The joy of one another.

The life we live
And love we give
Bring honor to our Mother.

Happy Mother's Day!

*Written on Mother's Day
in honor of all Mothers*

Bewitching

Just beyond our distant vision
Enchantment is at hand,
It's a land so captivating
That only children understand.

The magic of imagination
Beguiling are the games they play,
The joy of every generation
That played the games they play today.

Charming innocence of dreams
Magically their thoughts come true
To us a mystery, so it seems,
Their joyful magic once was you.

Robert F. Daniels

Blessings

Fireflies that wink at night
Light their way by lantern light
Chasing moonbeams in the sky;
They're so different from a butterfly.

The beauty of a butterfly
Reflecting color as he drifts by,
His splendor comes from sunbeams' light;
He never ever flies at night.

The joy and beauty day and night
Are God's gifts, and pure delight.
He shows he has a whimsical way,
His blessings grace us more each day.

Leaves

The flutter of the falling leaves
Drifting down from off the trees,
The beauty of an autumn scene
Splendored color so is seen
Floating on a gentle breeze.

The barren empty arms of trees
Starkly stand through winter's freeze
Reaching skyward, seem to pray
While remembering a warmer day,
Its days of glory and its leaves.

Bursting leaves on budding trees
Somehow gives them dignity,
The joy of spring as flowers bloom
Sprung from Mother Nature's womb
Brings beauty with that crown of leaves.

Halloween

If you ever take a walk
On a dark and gloomy night
You'll hear the goblins talk;
They'll always give you fright.

On Halloween the spooks and goblins are near,
Better watch the path you're takin'
Cuz they'll always give you fear.
They'll be watchin' you a-shakin'
And see your face turn white
And know they've got you worried
On that dark and dismal night.

You'll finally find a friendly light
When you were ready for defeat;
It will be your triumph of the night
When you shout out "Trick or Treat."

Fog

The fog is a mist,
The earth has been kissed
By the touch of a low flying cloud,
The comforting cover
Like the love of a Mother
Enclosing the earth like a shroud.

In the mists angels singing
God's love they are bringing
From Heaven for both you and me.
I remember their voices
Through the mists of our choices,
The sound of that sweet melody.

Robert F. Daniels

Jeff

He was rowdy and angry and quite often mean,
He was generous and loving as ever you've seen,
He was happy and funny and good for a joke,
His troubles were many and he'd always be broke.

Old cars and young folks and the game that run wild
Was his life and his love for he was God's child,
Independent and stubborn but always a man,
Desolation and loneliness, lost in the end.

He was helpful and kind and tried to do good,
He'll always be remembered and well that he should.
These thoughts and these memories are all we have left
Of the one we know as our youngest son Jeff.

Emerald Isle

Have you ever seen a small enchanted island
Filled with shamrocks and leprechauns at play?
Have you ever been across the sea to Dublin
Or watched the setting sun from Galway Bay?

Did you ever see the rainbows over Shannon
Where lilting voices raise in Irish song?
If you ever get a chance to visit Limerick
It's for that enchanting isle that I long.

If you can find the time to visit Derry
You'll see her cliffs that rise majestically.
They await like sentinals watching every
Fishing boat that floats on choppy seas.

When you get to Blarney and its famous stone
And see the lovers walk there hand in hand
The memories I've shared will then be your own
And then you'll know you've been to Ireland.

Robert F. Daniels

God's Love

The magnitude of the universe
That reaches beyond the realms of time,
Forever distant, time and space
Blessed by God's eternal grace;
Its vastness overwhelms the mind.

Imagine Heaven's magnificent size,
The universe is compromised,
God's creation magnified
And here on earth He lived and died.
But up there, with His heavenly view
The only place for all His love for you
Is the magnitude of the universe.

Schizophrenia

Chaotic minds confused and blurred,
The voice of reason goes unheard,
The torment of these tortured souls
Cast into their secluded holes.

A twisted life, half wrong half right,
Frantic fantasies and fright,
The step beyond is one thin line
And you could cross it any time.

Pondering

I am a tree,

Reaching limbs to touch the sky
While watching I am wondering why,
As I watch everything I dream
While overlooking a small stream,

I am a tree.

Birds are nesting in my crown
While I'm shading creatures on the ground.
I see the fish that swim and birds that fly
And I still am wondering why

I am a tree.

(continued)

A mighty oak for a hundred years
I overlook the hills and valley of tears,
A lonely sentry, I watch the sky
And while I watch I wonder why

I am a tree.

The birds and creatures come and go,
How they can travel, I don't know.
They come and go both near and far,
I wonder why things are as they are

I am a tree.

Robert F. Daniels

The Glory Of Our Lives

Seventy odd years of marriage my dear
And growing older together,
We've fought the battle of toil and tears
And we still have one another.

Loving and caring throughout all our years;
The joy we've known of life's sharing,
The wisdom we've gained, the laughter and tears
While we both know how much we're caring.

The pride of our children,
We aged as they grew,
The love of our family
That sprung from us two.

The grandchildren came
And then came the greats;
While each one is special
We all face our fates.

Soon I know that we'll have to part
And one of us will go to our rest.
You'll always be near me, close to my heart
While knowing that our lives were the best.

My Love To You

You add colors to the rainbows
And extra stars up in the skies,
You put glitter in the moon glow
With the magic of your eyes.

Moonlight and stardust are falling on me,
Rainbows and magic lead to my door,
Sunbeams and lovelight are the garments you see,
Happiness holds me forever more.
Our lives are entwined and always will be,
On earth and in Heaven it's you I adore.

Church Picnic

Horse shoes ring and children sing,
Music by our pastor.
Games and fun for old and young,
Rain would bring disaster.

Melodious songs led by the Strongs,
The pig from Kurzwiel meats,
Cakes and pies with great surprise
At the quantity of treats.

A gigantic feast blessed by our priest,
Visiting with friends,
There is joyous fun for everyone,
It's picnic time again.

Lost Love

The whistle of the train at night
Like the lonesome call of a dove in flight
As it rumbled down the railroad tracks
And the memories that come pouring back

Of another time in another place
And the haunting innocence of her face,
Her gentle voice and sweet caress
And the love that she shared with such tenderness.

Then the lunging urge of that mad stampede,
Chaos created by the rustlers' greed,
The thundering herd and her life was gone;
And I'm pondering now if I can still go on.

Robert F. Daniels

The Window Of My Mind

Drifting thoughts and memories
Floating past the window of my mind
Remind me of how it used to be
And of the woman I left home behind.

Will she be there when I get home again?
Knowing love will help me find the way
I'll ask her to forgive me for the pain,
I know I've hurt her more and more each day.

It's been so long, I've wandered far and wide
Across the land with every Rodeo,
A reckless life of glory for each ride
And full of pride I've faced each daily show.

It's been too long; I'm coming home once more.
My wandering life has now come to an end.
I'm just hoping that she'll love me as before
And take me back into her arms again.

Drifting thoughts and memories
Floating past the window of my mind
Remind me of how it used to be
And of the woman I left home behind.

The Rodeo Bull

Well, he came out of Texas, he was snakey and mean,
He was the ornerest bull that I'd ever seen.
He was blowin' smoke out of his nose
And his eyes shoot fire wherever he goes.
Well, I drew his ride at the buckin' pens
And if I'd had my choice, I'd have drawn again.

They finally got him into the chute
A-snortin' smoke out of his snoot.
He was jumpin' and kickin' and pawin' the ground
But the only face I saw was the rodeo clown.
He's the feller that will save my hide
If I expect to survive this ride.

We came out of that chute with a thunderin' cry
With that ol' bull a-jumpin' high in the sky.
He was buckin' and kickin' and spinnin' wide
While he kept on givin' a terrible ride.
At last I finally lost my grip
When he went and done a double backflip.

He made a pass as I hit the ground
And I grabbed his tail as he was comin' around.
Well, I set my heels and gave a mighty jerk
While the bull's momentum did the rest of the work.
Up he flew and I gave him a spin
And stacked him up 'gainst the loadin' pens.

The funniest sight I think I've seen
Was when I seen that ol' bull's face turn green.
I think I'll find me a new career;
I believe maybe I might have found one here
When I discovered I could throw that bull.
I want you folks to know I've just filled you full!

Robert F. Daniels

Memories

The joy of a child
When she kissed me and smiled,
The living and a-dying
The laughing and a-crying
The sorrow and the happiness and tears,

The loving and a-giving,
All the birthdays and Thanksgiving
The Christmases and Happy New Years,
And the innocence and trust of tender years,

Appreciating life. All the happiness
And Strife
And the memories in
December of my years.

Life

The living and a-dying the laughing and a-crying,
The sorrow and the happiness and tears,

The loving and a-giving, all the birthdays and Thanksgiving
The Christmases and Happy New Years,

The joy of a child as she kissed you and smiled,
The innocence and trust of tender years,

Appreciating life, all the happiness and strife,
And the memories in December of my years.

Robert F. Daniels

Summer

Thistle down and dragon flies,
Fire flies and summer skies,
Gentle breezes soft and warm
Emanate the season's charm.

Joyous times and lazy days,
Celebrating holidays,
Picnics in the local park,
Summer fun is such a lark.

Cook outs in the afternoon,
These summer days are gone too soon,
Cantaloupe and roasting ears
Memories to last another year.

Edged In Gold

Edged in gold, the letter told
Of wedding bells and joy,
Bells would ring and choirs sing
For a happy girl and boy.

The letter said to all who read:
The time, the date, the place,
Come and share with those who care
The occasion of flowers and lace.

The tarnished gold on letter's edge
Was like a knife, a final wedge
Destroying dreams of us together,
One broken heart, she's gone forever.

On Fish And Faces

The humility of a fish
Who spends his life in a transparent dish,
Chambered in a watery mass,
A prisoner in that world of glass.

Imagine a life of such a condition,
A life where fish go people fishin'
Caged within transparent bowls
And the leering faces of fishy ghouls.

Our Marriage

You and I, go our way
Joined as one forever.
We spoke the vows, on that day,
And start our lives together.
Tears were shed, in happiness
As you took my name,
Bells rang out and angels sang
As from the church we came.
Our wedding day has come and gone
Erased for all of time.
That was our start and not the end
For you'll be always mine.
A cloak of love and happiness
Shall hang about our door.
My very own, my precious wife
To cherish and adore.

Living Days

We're riding the great express ride of life,
Each day is a stop on the way.
Some days are happy and some days are glad,
It's like painting a picture of the best that you've had.
Some stops are lonely, hardship, and strife
But I want to remember each day of my life.

There's sorrow and happiness and days that you're down,
There's the humble, the tender, and the night on the town,
There's the feelin' of givin', the joy of just livin' –
Each adventure's a day just your own.

She's a wistful woman and her train ride is rough.
There's the good times and the bad times and when I've lived
long enough
I'll have one more stop, but I guess you'll be cryin'
When I meet with my maker at the end of the line.

There's sorrow and happiness and days that you're down,
There's the humble, the tender, and the night on the town,
There's the feelin' of givin', the joy of just livin' –
Each adventure's a day just your own.

Spring

HARK!
The form of winter old and weak,
The voice of spring begins to speak,
The gentle showers in the glen,
The birds begin to sing again –
HARK!
The April daffodils a-bloom
Sprung from Mother Nature's womb,
The softly blowing southern breeze,
The bursting leaves on budding trees –
HARK!
Spring removes the winter's yoke
And wears her own majestic cloak,
Dormant life begins to grow,
Sunshiny days replace the snow.

Robert F. Daniels

It's Wrong

It's wrong when you're with someone
To pretend you're in the arms of another.
It's wrong to act happy when you're lonesome,
When you're trying to forget an old lover.

I'm wrong, you're gone,
I'm lonesome and blue,
We quarreled and parted;
I'm lost without you.

How I long for the time we'll be together
And never again you'll be gone.
I'll love you my darling, forever;
Living without you is wrong.

Path Of Peace

Will a bird bring a branch from an Olive tree
As a sign of peace for the world to see?
Will the stars that gleam from the skies on high
Shine a light through the night to lead us by?
Can a dream survive in the hearts of men
Through the strife of their life to be born again?
Is the knell that we hear the dirge of doom?
Only hope can prevail through the darkest gloom.
Peace and hope is the song that our hearts sing
With our flag unfurled, let freedom ring.

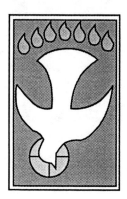

Tornado

Over yonder hangs a cloud
Black and deadly as a shroud
Reigning destruction as it blows
Leaving sorrow where'er it goes.
The day began as all the rest
And then — the darkness in the west.
The summer breeze began to swell,
Our Paradise turned into Hell.
The twisting funnel touched the ground
Destroying everything it found,
Farmland homes were wiped away,
Little children gone to play
Were caught before that summer gale,
Their lifeless bodies told the tale,
And other dead were in the path
Where Mother Nature spent her wrath.
The rain that followed mixed with tears
For loved ones lost and children, dear,
And later when the sun returned
A gleaming rainbow brightly burned
In mute respite it humbly spoke
Of nature's fury and sorrow's yoke.

Dawn

Dawn was just breaking
As I stepped into Paradise,
While the full moon was yawning
The sun began to rise.

The morn was reluctant
To accept the night's stillness;
The fresh mists enfolding
Wrapped me in their chilliness.

The mourning doves and sparrows
Seemed to wait in the silence
For the Master of Paradise
To lift them from their trance.

While the hoot owls in couples
Keep watch in the night
With faithful alertness
Until dawn's first light

The disinterest they have
For the lone figure nearby
Who is awed and spellbound
By the wonders on high.

Ah.......the glory God saves
For this sacred time of day,
The time just at dawn
Just as night slips away.

- Camille Dawn Angela Daniels
Sr. Clare Joseph, OCD

Forgiveness

I can remember my dad
when I could no more come to his knee;
A joyful smile so broad across his face,
his eyes as blue as the sea.

How handsome I thought he was;
I felt such safety in his presence,
Always full of tricks and stories
and pure goodness was his essence.

And then as I grew older
I developed ideas of my own.
So often I contradicted Dad
was my heart becoming stone?

He taught that I could do anything,
all I had to do was try;
Fall down again and again I would
"developing character" became my pie.

Dad always stood by my side
though during trials I would have denied this;
So blind I was to his unfaltering love
Filled with arrogance, my heart was amiss.

Many years and events have passed us by
and I thought I had made some progress;
but I find still deep within me
the same gross faults and self-centeredness.

Even when grace came
within my heart to abide,
My high demands and expectations
are the thorn within my side.

We are reminded of mercy and forgiveness,
gifts of love from our Lord and Savior;
And I ask of you, dear Dad,
to please forgive my unloving behavior.

By now you have probably shed
a tear or maybe two;
Not because of the words I have written,
though all of them are true.

But to learn that I did not inherit
your finesse with the written word;
Nonetheless, I love you today and always,
your daughter in Christ the Lord.

Camille Dawn Angela Daniels
Sr. Clare Joseph of the Sacred Heart
October 17, 2000

Robert F. Daniels

When A Grain Of Wheat Falls To The Ground

A grain of wheat
must fall to the earth;
it must first die
before it becomes what it's worth.

The soil is then nourished
with the sun and the rain;
the plants then burst forth
into a glorious field of grain!

A field that is most beautiful;
shining in the sun, it resembles pure gold.
Sending forth waves in the breeze,
this is a sight to behold!

The wheat is then removed from the field,
transformed into food, that which was seed.
Cereals and breads in abundance are made,
to nourish our bodies with all that we need.

This wheat is also made into another food;
true bread from above, that of our Lord.
When we eat this bread *In Remembrance of Him*,
our souls are then nourished, given strength and the sword.

I'm sure you were hoping
I was near to the end;
Almost, but not quite,
my father and friend.

From my childhood I cling to a memory -
walking with my sisters and brothers;
You showed us a field
which stood out from the others.

You walked straight to this wheat field
and told us to come;
You said "Here, if you chew this,
it will turn into gum."

I chewed and was amazed! -
this food on my tongue
Was straight from the earth;
the Glory of God forever is sung!

- Camille Dawn Angela Daniels
Sr. Clare Joseph, O.C.D.
February 1, 2001

My Own — "Hall Of Fame" favorite top ten

Jesus The Christ
Babe Ruth
Albert Einstein
Nat "King" Cole
Vince Lombardi
Mark Twain
Will Rogers
Joe Louis
John F. Kennedy
My Mother

Dreams, Joy, Faith, Love and Compassion
These are some of — "Life's Trails"

Robert F. Daniels

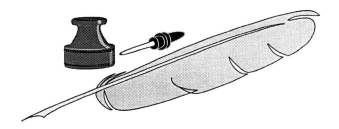

Index